LIFE ON
THE FARM

ANTHONY BURTON

IMPORTANT DATES

c. 4000 BC The first Neolithic farmers in Britain begin clearing the land to raise stock and grow crops.

AD 47 The Roman conquest of southern Britain: the Romans introduce water-powered grain mills.

1086–87 Domesday Book provides details of the English farming landscape.

c. 1200 Heavy horses introduced for ploughing.

1348 The start of the Black Death reduces England's population by a third and results in much arable land being turned to pasture.

1623 Cornelius Vermuyden begins the first of a series of schemes for the drainage of the fens in East Anglia.

1701 Jethro Tull invents the seed drill.

1720 The start of a period of extensive enclosure of common land and open fields, each of which require a separate Enclosures Act.

1760 Sheep introduced into the Scottish Highlands and the start of the Highland Clearances.

1785 Robert Ransome takes out a patent for a plough with cast iron shares.

1786 Successful threshing drum invented by Andrew Meikle.

1800 Richard Trevithick invents a portable steam engine that can be used to power a threshing machine.

1831 American Cyrus McCormick invents a mechanical reaper that is soon widely used in Britain.

1834 Six Dorset farm workers arrested for forming a trades union: they become known as the Tolpuddle Martyrs.

1841 Robert Ransome demonstrates the first steam traction engine.

1842 John Bennet Lawes takes out a patent for the manufacture of 'superphosphate' fertilizers.

1858 The Royal Agricultural Society awards John Fowler a prize for his successful steam plough.

1886 Crofters' Act passed, protecting Scottish crofters from eviction by landlords.

1889 The Charter Gas Engine Company of Chicago introduces the first internal combustion engine tractor.

1908 Formation of the National Farmers Union.

1943 Production of the synthetic pesticide DDT begins.

1972 Foundation of the International Federation of Organic Agriculture Movements.

2000 First full-scale trials of genetically modified crops in Britain.

SIX THOUSAND YEARS OF HISTORY

Somewhere around 4000 BC, people in Britain began to give up their old way of life as hunter-gatherers and began using stone axes to clear the forest to make permanent settlements. Here they began raising livestock and planting crops: they became farmers. We know something of their way of life: archaeologists have discovered that their fields were not ploughed in the sense that we understand it – their light ploughs did little more than scratch the surface; we know from the remains of bones that show marks of butchering that their cattle were huge beasts, closely related to the wild aurochs, but their sheep were quite small; and from one remarkable site we can get an idea of their domestic life. Skara Brae on Orkney, off the north-east tip of Scotland, was abandoned when it was covered by a sandstorm but reappeared in another storm in 1850. This little cluster of houses still have their furnishings, which include box-beds made of stone slabs that could have been filled with heather, a central cooking area and what can only be described as stone dressers. The remains show that they grew barley, kept livestock and fished, rather like later generations of crofters.

The Stone Age gave way to the Bronze Age, c. 2000 BC. Grimspound in Devon is a cattle farm from that period, the remains of which show a number of circular hut dwellings contained within a substantial granite wall. Celtic fields from this time and the later Iron Age can be found in many upland areas of Britain, on moors and downland. They show a pattern of small, square fields, surrounded by high banks in which the soil was broken up by ploughing once in one direction, then again at right angles to the first furrows.

Following the invasion of AD 47, the Romans brought one major change to British farmers. Previously grain had been ground by hand, using simple stone devices called querns, but the newcomers built grain mills powered by waterwheels. The available tools and technologies of prehistoric farmers may have been primitive, but the pattern of life, sowing and harvesting, stock rearing and tending, had all the basic elements of farming through the ages.

One of the houses in the Neolithic farming settlement at Skara Brae, Orkney. The drystone walls were well constructed, and the original stone furniture, including this 'dresser', is well preserved.

THE MEDIEVAL FARM

▲ A new hedge being laid in Oxfordshire, c. 1950s. The fields now used for grazing have the typical corrugated pattern of ridge and furrow, showing that they were ploughed in medieval times.

In the upland regions of Britain, especially the Celtic lands of Wales and Scotland, farming continued much as it had for many centuries, but there were major changes in the lowland areas that began with the Anglo Saxons and continued into the period following the Norman conquest of 1066.

This was a period dominated by farming settlements, rather than isolated farms, and of the open field system. In general, the open field was divided into strips, each roughly 220 yards (200m) long, a furrow's length that later became the standard measurement known as the furlong. The strips were shared out between the various peasant farmers of the settlement. Teams of oxen were used for ploughing, and the plough turned the earth to one side, creating a ridge. On the return, the earth was heaped on top of the first ridge.

The result was a pattern of high ridges where the seed was sown by hand, alternating with deep furrows that ensured good drainage. In later years some of these fields were grassed over, preserving the pattern that can still be seen today. After the harvest the fields were thrown open to all the farmers for their stock to graze the stubble, and every two or three years a field would be left fallow, ploughed but not sown, to recover the necessary nutrients used up by the crops. The management of the fields was mainly left to the community, who held regular meetings to decide matters such as allocation of strips and settlement of disputes.

SERFS AND LORDS

These peasant farmers were nearly all serfs, owing allegiance to the lord of the manor: they were forced to spend a certain number of days every

◄ An illustration from the 14th-century Holkham Bible showing ploughing with oxen being led by a donkey, while a man sows seed in the background.

year working on the lord's land; all their grain had to be ground in the lord's mill; and they were not allowed to leave their holdings. They even required the lord's consent for their children to get married. They did, however, enjoy certain rights, of which the most important was the use of common land. The woods provided timber for building and fuel for their fires; they could gather all kinds of food, from herbs and mushrooms to rabbits and birds caught in snares. In addition, open land could be used for grazing.

The cottages the peasant farmers lived in were very basic. The building materials depended on what was available locally. Where building stone was scarce the structures would be timber-framed, the spaces between filled with wattle (interlacing twigs) and the whole covered with daub (a clay mixture). The roof was of thatch and generally everything happened in the single room, lit during the day by unglazed windows that could be closed off with shutters. These very simple houses have not survived, but contemporaries have left descriptions of them. The fire that was used for heat and cooking was generally set in the centre of the room, with the smoke escaping through a hole in the thatch – though according to Bishop Hall, writing in the 16th century, it still did not prevent the beams being 'furred with sluttish soote a whole inch thick'. At night the family would share the space with livestock; Bishop Hall described them as

sleeping with cattle at their feet, pigs under the bed and hens perching on the rafters.

Eventually the feudal way of life began to break down. Following the terrible years of the Black Death in the 14th century, when a third of the population died, labour became scarce and the peasants were in a better bargaining position. Serfdom and subsistence farming gave way to a new system in which the labourers were paid in cash. Farming was about to enter a new era.

▲ Barns such as this scarcely changed in design over many centuries.

THE AGRICULTURAL REVOLUTION

The dissolution of the monasteries (1536–40) by Henry VIII made large tracts of land available, which passed to new, wealthy owners. They had no need to share their property with others, so the old open fields were no longer needed, and they could build themselves far grander farmhouses, complete with such 'modern' innovations as chimneys, and with separate areas for livestock. By the 17th century, Britain was enjoying a new prosperity, briefly interrupted by the Civil War (1642–51), and one feature was a movement of large numbers of the population from the countryside to the town. The feudal system had worked well enough in its day, but now farms needed to become more productive to feed a growing urban population. One route to improvement was to enclose the old commons and turn them into privately owned fields. For a hundred years or more from the 1720s, Parliament passed a series of Enclosure Acts, which made improvement possible but deprived the peasant farmers of their old rights.

CHANGING TIMES

Enclosures and schemes such as the drainage of the East Anglia fens increased the area of land available for growing crops, and new methods made them more productive. Horses had already begun to

replace oxen for working the farm as early as the 13th century, but otherwise changes had been few. In the 18th century the pace of development began to quicken, starting with the introduction of lighter, more efficient ploughs, based on ideas developed in Holland. The most important advances, however, came with changes in the types of crops and the ways in which they were grown. Two new crops, turnips and clover, were especially important. Their use is particularly associated with 'Turnip' Townshend, or, as he was more formally known, Charles, 2nd Viscount Townshend. Instead of allowing fields to lie fallow so that they could be weeded and allowed to recover, he planted them with these two crops. Seed for grain crops such as wheat had been broadcast, spread out haphazardly by hand. The turnip seeds were sown in regular rows and evenly spaced, so that weeds could easily be cleared by hoeing. Clover was

◄ In the 13th century, horses were being introduced to take over farm work from oxen – a tradition that continued for around 600 years.

◀ The enclosure of the old open fields and commons led to the familiar farming landscape of squared fields like these in Nottinghamshire.

▼ Improved livestock breeding produced splendid animals, and proud farmers often paid local artists to have themselves painted with their prize bulls,

STEALING THE LAND

Otmoor in Oxfordshire was an area of waterlogged wasteland, where people from the surrounding villages traditionally grazed a few sheep, but also kept large flocks of geese. In 1815 it was enclosed, but local people felt that they had lost valuable ancient rights. Their views were expressed in a local poem of the period:

> The fault is great in Man or Woman
> Who steals the Goose from off a Common;
> But who can plead that man's excuse
> Who steals the Common from the Goose?

In 1830 the area erupted in riots, in which fences were pulled down and hedges destroyed: the unrest lasted for four years.

of Dishley, Leicestershire. He was responsible for the famous Leicester sheep, Dishley longhorn cattle and a new breed of black heavy horse that worked exceptionally well in harness on the farm. He established the Dishley Club to register new breeds and ensure purity of the bloodline, and hired out his prize rams and bulls to other farmers. He was so successful that the hiring programme was earning him as much as £3,000 a year, over £2 million at today's value.

invaluable in introducing nitrogen to the soil: we now know that this is due to bacteria on the roots turning nitrogen in the air into nitrates. By rotating crops over a four-year period – turnips, barley or oats, clover, wheat – Townshend never had to leave his land to lie fallow and unproductive.

The new farmers were able to keep their stock isolated within their own fields, and began programmes of selective breeding. The foremost stockbreeder was Robert Bakewell (1725–95)

▲ New devices were introduced, such as this 17th-century horse-powered mill, which was still in a Haverfordwest farm in Wales in the 1930s.

▲ Ploughing with horses; at the end of the working day this farmer would ride home on the pair.

The great change in ploughing came in the 18th and early 19th centuries with the gradual replacement of the wooden plough by ones made of iron. There was a problem with the first iron ploughs in that the share that did the cutting tended to lose its edge. In 1785 Robert Ransome, working in a foundry in Norwich, took out a patent for chilled cast iron shares, in which one side was softer than the other, so that it always wore out first, exposing more of the opposite side – in effect making it self-sharpening. He went on to establish his own firm and manufactured ploughs with inter-changeable parts.

➤ Seed could be sowed more evenly by the use of a seed fiddle than if scattering by hand.

THE HORSEMAN'S DAY

The horseman who looked after the horses always ensured that they were kept in excellent condition, well groomed with their tails neatly plaited. His day could start as early as 4 a.m., for the horses had to

be fed and harnessed and ready for work by 7 a.m.. William Stephens, a 14-year-old ploughboy, described his working life in the 1860s. He would work through until about 11 in the morning, when he would have a meal break, usually bread and cheese washed down with cider – he was allowed three pints (1.5 litres) a day. The work would continue until about 4 p.m., by which time he would

After ploughing, the soil is broken up by harrowing.

Before the arrival of artificial fertilizers, the ground was improved by muck spreading – covering the ground with farmyard manure.

have ploughed about three-quarters of an acre (0.3 ha). It was not the end of the working day, though. The horses had to be taken back to the stable, fed and settled down for the night. The priority was clear: the horses always came first. Only when they had been properly tended could young William get home, usually by about 7.30 p.m., for his evening meal, and it was not long after 8 o'clock that he was in his bed and sound asleep.

It was not just the hard work of tramping all day behind the plough that made the job arduous. There was also the need to concentrate all the time, in order to keep a straight furrow, keeping the plough running along beside the previous furrow and controlling the horses. As anyone who has ever ploughed with horses will confirm, this is not an easy task and the good ploughman took pride in his work.

HARROWING AND SOWING

Originally, clods of earth would have been broken up after ploughing by using simple tools such as mattocks, which was back-breaking work. The introduction of the harrow, an iron frame set with iron teeth, that would be dragged over the ground by horses, made life easier for the labourers.

When the ground had been prepared, the seed was sown. Broadcast sowing was done by hand, the sower carrying the seed in a basket slung over his shoulder and casting the seed to either side, the action of his hand keeping pace with the rhythm of his stride. It was somewhat haphazard, and uneven sowing meant an uneven crop. An early improvement was the seed fiddle which, as the name suggests, used a vibrating string to throw out the seed. By the late 17th century it had been recognized that sowing seed into regular holes produced a more even crop, and in 1701 Jethro Tull, a law student from Berkshire who was forced by ill health to abandon his profession and take up farming, invented the seed drill. The seed box was mounted on a wheeled carriage: after drilling the hole, the seeds were dropped down a grooved cylinder, controlled by a spring-loaded tongue. Using the original version, a horse could drill three rows of seeds at a time.

PRIDE IN HIS WORK

Arthur Chaplin, a ploughman in 19th century Suffolk, wrote: 'As soon as you had a break in your ploughing you'd walk along the headlings to have a look at your neighbour's work, to see where he had gone, or if his ploughing was better than yours. It wouldn't do just to have straight furrows: a good ploughman also had to have a good top to the stetch [group of furrows] – the furrows lying all flat and even.'

HARVESTING

Harvest time was the busiest time of the year on the farm. It was essential to make the most of fine weather to get the crop in, and men, women and children would be out in the fields from dawn to dusk. In many regions, the farmers had to negotiate rates with a representative of the field hands, known as the 'Lord of the Harvest'. In the 18th century, the grain was cut using sickles and hooks, and in East Anglia it was customary for the farmer to pay 'glove money', or even hand out gloves to protect the hands of the workers. By the 19th century the sickle had largely been replaced by the scythe and the first attempts to design mechanical reapers were being made. Although the first patent in Britain was taken out in 1800, it was not until 1826 that a Scots inventor, Patrick Bell (1799–1869), came up with a really practical machine. Bell was a minister of the church, but he had been brought up on his father's farm; his only reason to tackle the problem was to relieve the heavy labour of the field workers. He never took out a patent,

▲ Reaping with a scythe: at harvest time there would be large numbers of reapers in every field.

hoping this would make the machine more widely available. It was unusual in that instead of being pulled by horses, it was pushed. Flailing blades called sails pushed the stalks down towards the cutters, which operated like giant scissors. Although the machine worked, it never came into general use. The big breakthrough was not a British invention, but the work of an American, Cyrus McCormick (1809–84), who in

▲ The first commercially successful reaping machine, made in America by McCormick's.

CORN DOLLIES

In Britain, corn dollies were traditionally fashioned from the last sheaf of wheat, or other cereal crop, of a harvest. This custom is likely to date from pagan times: one story is that the corn spirit, made homeless during harvesting, could winter in the corn dolly, which was then ploughed into the first furrow at the turn of the season.

∧ The art of making corn dollies was passed down through generations of farming families.

was done using flails, an unpleasant and unhealthy job as the men working in an enclosed space were surrounded by clouds of dust.

Haymaking was similar to reaping, but where the hay was not kept in barns, it had to be protected from the elements by making into haystacks, which were then covered by thatch. The end of harvesting was a time of celebration and also a time for gleaning. The farmers would allow the workers, usually women and children, onto the fields of stubble to gather as much grain as they could. Barley would be used to feed a pig or chickens, and wheat would be ground into flour. This was an important item in the labourer's budget: a government survey found that an Oxfordshire labourer in 1893 was earning 14s 4½d a week (around 72p), of which 6 shillings (30p) went on bread and flour. It is no wonder that women would stay on in the fields for weeks after the harvest in order to glean every grain they could to help see them through the winter months.

1831 developed a machine not dissimilar to Bell's, but which was pulled instead of pushed. In 1847 McCormick moved from Virginia to Chicago, where he established a factory to make his machines; these were shown at the 1851 exhibition at Crystal Palace, London, and were soon making an appearance in British fields.

JOBS FOR ALL AGES

Mechanical reapers did not mean an end to the hard work of harvesting. Children were given the job of making bands out of wheat straw, which were then used by the women to bind the sheaths, which in turn were arranged into stooks by the men. There was a constant movement of carts to and from the fields which took the corn to the barn for threshing, separating the wheat grains from the chaff. Throughout the 18th century this

∧ Men and women working together to build a haystack.

Cattle could be kept as dairy herds or for meat – the roast beef of England was so famous in the 18th century that the French knew the British as '*les rosbifs*'. The life of the dairyman was governed by the hours of milking. When the cows were milked in sheds in the farmyard, the day started with fetching them from the field, often as early as 4 or 5 o'clock in the morning. It was a slow amble for the beasts, whose udders were heavy with milk, and they were not to be hurried. It was not unusual on many farms, however, for the animals to be milked in the field by hand. It could be a pleasant occupation on a fine, sunny summer morning. It was very different in cold, wet winter weather. The cowman would tramp out in heavy boots and gaiters and the warmest coat he owned, set down his three-legged stool on ground usually covered in mud and manure, and there he stayed for two hours or more with his head pressed against the cold, wet flanks of the beasts. Milking over, he would trudge back to the farm for a well-deserved breakfast. The process then had to be repeated in the afternoon.

▲   Milking by hand in the byre.

MORE THAN MILKING

Milking was only a part of the cowman's work. He was responsible for the movement of the animals from field to field to ensure there was always good grazing. He also had to be responsible for their welfare and, during the calving season, would often be up all night ensuring a cow had a safe delivery.

In upland areas, where grazing was harder to come by, the farmers had to adopt very different systems. In the Scottish Highlands, the herds were turned out onto the hills in spring and the herdsman would go with them, living in a hut known as a shieling, generally built of rough stone walls covered by a thatched roof and with just a single room. This allowed the fields in the valley to be used to grow hay or root vegetables for winter feed. In the Yorkshire Dales farmers

THE DAIRYMAN

Many dairymen had other duties and privileges. A.H. Bonditch worked on a Dorset farm in the 1890s. He was paid £1 a week for looking after 28 cows, and had a rent-free cottage. He also looked after pigs and poultry, and his wife made butter and cheese. For this he got '5 per cent at the end of the year on all clear profit made on Butter, Cheese & Pigs'.

A demonstration of the latest dairy equipment by the Yorkshire County Council Dairy School, c. 1900.

Delivering milk in churns by horse and cart.

developed a system of field barns. All along the floor of the dale, the ground would be divided up into fields, each with its own barn. During the summer months, while the animals were out on the moor, the hay would grow in the fields and after harvesting would be loaded into the upper floors of the barn. In winter it could be dropped from the hayloft to the beasts below, and their manure would be cleared out to spread on the fields, ready for the new seasons' growth.

In the 18th century, all milk was consumed locally, either being drunk or made into butter and cheese. The coming of the railways in the 19th century meant that the farmer could serve a larger area. Milk was poured into churns, which were collected in carts and taken down to the nearest station to be ready for the early morning

Cattle being driven to market in Newport, Shropshire.

trains to the towns. Milking times were often tied to railway timetables.

Before refrigeration, the only way to get fresh meat to the customers was to bring it to market on the hoof. The drovers would travel immense distances with their herds to get the best possible price. A 17th-century writer recorded that three thousand head of cattle were sent to England from distant Anglesey, while as many as thirty thousand came through mid-Wales to Hereford. Mounted on ponies, the drovers might have cattle strung out along half a mile (0.8km) of the road.

It was not only cattle that were driven to market: this flock of geese is being taken through the streets of Darlington.

▲ Shepherd Septimus Liddle, *c.* 1940.

Sheep have played a hugely important part in the story of Britain's agriculture, valued not as they are now for their flavour as tender lamb, but for their fleece. English wool was traded all over Europe in vast quantities. One Tuscan merchant, Francesco di Marco Datini, imported 40,000lbs (18,000kg) of English wool into his Genoa warehouse in 1397. The monasteries kept huge flocks: in the 13th century the Abbey of Gloucester had 10,000 sheep roaming the Cotswold hills. By 1600 it was estimated that there were five times as many sheep in England as there were people. There were two main varieties: the short-woolled sheep that lived on the poorer pastures such as the Yorkshire moors and the chalk downlands, of which the Ryeland was the most valued, famous for its fine wool; the long-woolled sheep thrived on lusher pastures and none was finer than the

Cotswold, known from its majestic appearance as 'the Cotswold Lion'. Wool made merchants rich, and the wealth can still be seen in the grand houses of the Cotswolds or the magnificent churches of East Anglia.

ONE MAN AND HIS DOG

The life of the shepherd was often lonely, spent out on the moor or downs, with only his dog for company. But the shepherd was regarded in many ways as the aristocrat of farm labourers, not least for the skill with which he trained his dog and the way in which they worked in perfect harmony. One shepherd, Frank Whatley, who began his working life as a boy in Wiltshire in the latter part of the 19th century, won a wager by getting his dog to round up 20 sheep in the eye of the White Horse, carved out of the hillside at Westbury.

The busiest time of the year was lambing, when men such as Whatley lived out on the downs in temporary huts erected for the season. He would often be up all night, helping the ewes and moving the newborn lambs and their mothers

▲ A shepherd and his sheepdog herd their flock in the Yorkshire Dales.

▲ Washing sheep ready for shearing: the stream has been dammed to ensure a good depth of water.

into temporary enclosures made out of hurdles. It was a time fraught with problems, and highly dependent on the vagaries of the British climate; many lambs could not survive if born in a period of cold, lashing rain. In a particularly bad year, Benjamin Coleman, who shared the responsibility of tending the flock with Frank Whatley, was heard to exclaim: 'Oh maister, it'll kill I!'

SHEARING TIME

The other frantic time of the year came at shearing time, just before the start of lambing. The sheep had to be washed in a suitable stream, dammed to create a pool. Usually two men stood up to their waists in the water, dragging the sheep in, while a third shepherd on the bank would use his crook to completely submerge the animals or to help them out if the weight of the wet fleeces were dragging them down. There was generally a two-week wait before the actual shearing began. Until the 20th century all shearing was done by hand, and a good shearer worked with exceptional speed; grabbing the sheep and clasping it firmly between his legs, he could have a fleece off in minutes. The world record for hand-shearing sheep was set in 1892, when one man sheared 321 sheep in just 7 hours 40 minutes.

▲ Shearing sheep using hand shears.

STEAM POWER ON THE FARM

The steam engine had been around for a century before it was introduced into farming, largely because for most of the 18th century there was no farm machinery to which it could be applied. That changed in 1786 when Scotsman Andrew Meikle invented the threshing drum. The drum rotated at high speed inside a concave plate, with just a small gap between the two. The cereal was fed in at the top and a rubbing action removed the grain. Rich farmers built special threshing mills, where the drums were turned by teams of horses. The agriculturist Arthur Young visited Oxfordshire in 1813 and reported that Lord Macclesfield's mill had cost £120 for the machinery alone, and needed four horses to make it work. Here was a suitable job for a steam engine, but there was a snag. The engines of the day were enormous machines, mainly because they worked using very low-pressure steam. This was the system preferred by the steam pioneer James Watt and as he held an all-embracing patent no developments were possible until it expired in 1800.

TREVITHICK'S SOLUTION

A young Cornish engineer, Richard Trevithick, was an enthusiastic advocate of small high-pressure engines that could do the work of one of the old

A portable steam engine, which would have been pulled into the field by horses, working a threshing drum.

giants. In 1812 he built an engine for use with a threshing machine for Sir Christopher Hawkins of Trewithen, near Truro. An independent test showed that it threshed 1,500 sheaves of barley in four and three-quarter hours and that the running cost was 2s 6d (12.5p) a day compared with £1 a day for horses. The steam cylinder was just 9 inches (23cm) in diameter, compared with the cylinder on a Watt engine that could be several feet across – small enough, in fact, for Trevithick to mount his engines on wheels. It was this idea that would eventually develop into the familiar traction engine.

By putting the engine and the threshing drum on wheels, the whole operation could be carried out in the fields. The engines were very similar to early locomotives, but with an important difference – they could not move themselves. They had to be hauled into place by teams of horses. Even when they were made to move themselves, there was a fundamental difficulty: they were almost impossible to steer, so horses still had to be harnessed to the front and controlled by reins. It was Thomas Aveling, a Cambridgeshire farmer

Before the invention of the threshing drum, the wheat had to be separated from the chaff by beating with flails.

▲ A threshing team with their engine, machinery and the van in which they would live throughout the harvest season, photographed c. 1890.

who discovered he had a flair for engineering, who developed the first engine that dispensed with horses altogether, but it was not until the 1860s that the modern traction engine with its steering wheel came into general use.

Although most farmers could not afford to install permanent engine-houses, many could afford to hire a traction engine and thresher to be brought to the farm. Teams were formed who toured the country at harvest time, taking with them a 'living van' (like a basic caravan) where they could sleep and have their meals.

PLOUGHING BY STEAM

The heavy traction engines could not take over the work done by horses for jobs such as ploughing, as the machines caused too much damage to the land. It was a Yorkshireman, John Fowler, who devised the first really successful steam ploughing system. It required two traction engines, each fitted with cable drums. The cable was attached to a balanced plough, with two sets of shares. The engines were positioned at each side of the field and the plough pulled across from one side to the other, after which both engines moved forward, and the plough was pulled back to make the next furrow. In the 20th century, the traction and ploughing engines were gradually replaced by tractors which, being much lighter, did not damage the land.

➤ Ploughing by steam: the ploughshares that are raised on this run will be lowered to the ground for the return to cut the next furrow.

CROFTING

The defeat of Bonnie Prince Charlie and his followers at the Battle of Culloden in 1746 marked the beginning of a period of great poverty for the people of the Highlands and Islands of Scotland. The old clan system was coming to an end and a new generation of often-absentee landlords began looking for more profitable ways of using the land than letting it to individuals at very low rents to tend small patches of ground or raise cattle on the common land. Vast areas were given over to sheep or were left as estates for game, and the people who had previously lived there were evicted – sometimes with great violence – and their homes destroyed. It was known as the Highland Clearances, an infamous period in the country's history, which saw many families forced into emigration. Those who remained mainly made their living as crofters.

THE LIFE OF A CROFTER

Crofters were basically self-sufficient. They grew crops, such as potatoes, barley and oats, and kept cattle on land shared out between a number of families. Those who lived near the coast usually kept boats for fishing, and in the islands it was not unusual for them to take sheep or cattle onto uninhabited islands for grazing: the sheep were carried in the boat, the cattle swimming alongside.

Croft houses in the 19th century were very simple, usually with stone walls, built without mortar, and a thatched roof made out of turf, covered in straw. Once the straw had been laid it was held in place by ropes. Living space consisted of no more than a single room lit by small windows. The open fire, fed with peat that

▼ A typical Shetland croft: it is not difficult to imagine how hard it must have been to earn a living in this rugged landscape.

▲ The interior of a very basic croft. A cooking pot is hung over the central, open fire and a spinning wheel is seen to the left.

▲ Women feeding hens outside a croft, c. 1900.

had been cut from the land and dried, was used for both heating and cooking. There was no chimney and the smoke had to make its way out where it could. Box-beds provided both privacy and warmth in winter, though they could be claustrophobic and hot in summer. The farm buildings consisted of a barn and a byre, sometimes attached to the house, and many crofts also had their own kilns for drying grain.

➤ Children bringing back peat for the fire at a Shetland croft, c. 1900.

AN ORKNEY CROFTER

A typical story from the 1884 Napier report tells of a farmer from Rousay, Orkney, who took previously uncultivated land and 'got up with much trouble a humble cottage and outhouses'. He worked the land by ditching and draining it until it was fit to grow crops but saw no benefit from all his hard work, saying: 'As I improved, more and more rent was laid on until I am now rented at a sum which is five times the rent I paid at first for a house I built myself.'

THE CROFTERS' ACT

Few crofters owned the land they worked, and in the 19th century they were often subjected to high rents that were either paid in cash or, more often, in produce. Not surprisingly, many left the land and even the country, forced out by poverty. The Highland Land League was formed in 1883 to pressurize Parliament to do something for the crofters. The following year a committee was set up under Baron Francis Napier to enquire into the situation, and as a result of their findings the Crofters' Act was passed in 1886. For the first time, the crofters had the protection of the law against the landlords, who could no longer evict them or subject them to arbitrary rent increases. They were finally secure in their homes and free to work their land.

The life of a farmer's wife was rarely easy. As well as the household chores common to all housewives, she was expected to do her share of the farm work, particularly at harvest time. For much of the year, however, her most important work often took place in the dairy, making butter and cheese. This was hard but important work that not only helped to feed the family but also added to their income.

BUTTER AND CHEESE

Buttermaking in the 19th century was much as it had been for centuries. First the milk was poured into shallow pans, and when the cream had risen to the surface it was skimmed off and churned, either by agitating with a plunger or by rotating it in a revolving barrel. Whichever system was used it required strong arms and considerable stamina. Once the cream had solidified, it had to be kneaded by hand to remove all the last traces of moisture. Cheesemaking, too, was very traditional, with each region producing its own variety; it could be made with ewes' milk and goats' milk as well as the more familiar cows' milk. The milk would originally have been allowed to sour

▲ The interior of this comfortable Essex farmhouse was photographed in the 1950s, although in other areas, even at this late date, many farms still had no mains services and used an open fire to boil the kettle.

naturally but it was discovered that the process could be speeded up and controlled by the addition of rennet, made from the lining of a calf's fourth stomach: in recent times vegetable-based rennets have also been introduced. The milk was warmed, the rennet added and, after half an hour or more, solids began to separate out. They had to be cut up using 'knives' that were actually small-mesh screens, and constantly stirred – many farmers found a hay rake ideal for this job. It was a matter of fine judgement to decide just when the process was complete. Next the liquid whey was run off, but not wasted – pigs found it a great treat. The curd was then removed and cut into blocks that were piled on top of each other and pressed down, a process that was repeated over and over again until the curd was dry enough to be wrapped in cloth and put in a press to complete the process.

CHILDREN ON THE FARM

Children in rural communities were expected to start work at an early age. The famous radical writer William Cobbett, born in 1763, recalled his own childhood as being hard but idyllic. He wrote:

▲ Churning butter by hand.

▲ Men and boys take a break from harvesting, and enjoy a joke. The boy with the gun would have shot rabbits as they ran from the stooks.

'I do not remember a time when I did not earn my living.' As a young boy he started out in the morning 'with my wooden bottle and my satchel over my shoulder'. His first job was scaring birds off the turnip seeds and the peas, and from there he graduated to weeding wheat and 'leading a single horse in harrowing barley'. His proudest day came when he could join the reapers in the field and drive a team of horses.

Others were less fortunate. There was often not enough work to keep all the children busy, so they

▲ The farmer's wife brings refreshment to field workers at harvest time.

were sent away to other farms, where they worked for a pittance but received their board and lodging. They were lucky if they were treated as well as they had been in their own homes.

A HARD LIFE

Richard Hillyer was sent away from home as a young boy in the 19th century to work on a farm. It was a miserable existence: 'Every night I dropped asleep over my supper, and then woke up just enough to crawl upstairs and fall into bed … A black depression spread over me. "This is what it is going to be from now on," I thought, "Lifting, hauling, shoving, trudging about from day to day, nothing else through all the years."'

THE FARM LABOURER

▲ Placing the coping stones: the finishing touches are added to a drystone wall in Derbyshire.

Following the spread of enclosures in the 18th and 19th centuries, many families who had once had their own patches of land and grazing rights on the common were forced to work as labourers on other men's farms. By the middle of the 19th century there were estimated to be one and a half million farm workers in England alone. How they lived and worked varied greatly from region to region. In the north of England, for example, it was common practice for the worker to live in the farmhouse, sharing his meals with the family and sleeping in a garret. In the south, workers were more likely to live in their own cottages, rented from the farmer. Wages were often low and living conditions miserable, but many farmers allowed their tenants to tend small plots of land to grow vegetables and to keep a pig. The pig would be treated more or less as a pampered pet, but there was no sentimentality involved. Even the smallest children knew what its fate would be: cured bacon and ham hung from the rafters in many cottage kitchens. Even these benefits failed to raise some families to anything approximating to a reasonable standard of living. There was little they could do, and when a group of labourers in Dorset attempted to band together in 1834 to form a

A SOUND WALL

An old waller in the Yorkshire Dales recalled being taught the craft by his father in about 1920. At the end of each day his father would take a few paces, run at the wall and give it a kick with all the force he could muster. If none of the stones shifted and there was no rattle from loose fillers on the inside then 'he would say it was well filled and sound'.

∧ At 80 years old James Capstick is seen here instructing his young nephew in the art of hedge laying in the Lune Valley, Lancashire.

union to press for better wages, magistrates found them guilty of being 'ill-disposed persons' under the terms of an obscure Act of 1797 and sentenced them to deportation to Australia. They have become famous in history as the Tolpuddle Martyrs.

DRYSTONE WALLING

The long days of spring and summer were always busy, changing with the seasons from ploughing and sowing to harvesting. During the rest of the year there were always maintenance jobs to keep everyone busy. Maintaining field boundaries was important. Where stone was plentiful the most common way to enclose a field was with drystone walls, and building them was not just a matter of piling rocks on top of each other in a haphazard fashion. Different areas used different techniques. For example, wall construction in the Pennines involved first digging a trench and lining it with two rows of squared boulders, after which the space between was filled with irregular stones, the whole forming a sound foundation. This same pattern was followed in building up the wall, with two outer layers of the best stones and an infilling. Longer stones – 'throughs' – were set at regular intervals to bind the wall together, and sometimes allowed to protrude to form the steps of a stile. The wall was then finished off with coping stones.

HEDGING AND DITCHING

Where stone was not available, hedges were the best alternative and, as with walling, there were real skills involved in producing a sound hedge.

Hedging was a winter job, a time when the leaves had fallen and the hedger could see what he was doing. Left to themselves, the shrubs, such as hawthorn, will grow upwards and straggle out. To keep a hedge to a uniform height and thickness, with no gaps that can be exploited by livestock interested in what might be happening in the next field, the hedge had to be laid. The tall shoots were bent over until almost horizontal and then partially cut through from the top surface, which made them grow in that direction. The wound would heal, and the branch would throw out prickly vertical shoots to make a suitably dense barrier. Hedges were often accompanied by ditches, which acted as barriers and drains. Ditching was invariably hard and unpleasant work, digging out silt and clay from freezing cold water.

∧ Agricultural students discovering that ditching involves hard, uncomfortable work as well as skill.

Not everyone in the farming community worked on the land, but their work was a vital part of the rural economy.

THE MILLER

One of the most important figures in agricultural life was the miller. The grain mill powered by a waterwheel was first introduced into Britain by the Romans, and became a vital part of the rural economy. The 11th-century Domesday Book survey listed an astonishingly large number of mills: 5,624 of them in England south of the River Trent. The watermill represented a major breakthrough in technology at the time, though now we think of it as old fashioned and rather quaint. The simplest type of waterwheel is the

Norse wheel, introduced from Scandinavia, that has blades mounted on a vertical axle and set right in the stream. As the axle rotates, it moves the attached grindstone inside the mill. The Roman wheel, however, was vertical, so in order to make grindstones turn horizontally it had to be fitted with gearing.

Millstones do not squash the grain, they slice it. The stones are 'dressed' – cut with a complex pattern of grooves that move over each other, like shears. The miller had to be constantly on the alert to ensure that the stones moved evenly at the correct rate to produce a consistent flow of flour of regular consistency. This might mean adjusting the sluice gates to control the flow of water, or adjusting the distance between the stones. When the windmill was introduced in the medieval period the miller had an extra job. The mill only works when the sails are facing into the wind, and winds change direction. In the first mills, the working machinery was housed in the buck, rather like a very large garden shed, mounted on a central post. To move the sails into the wind, the miller had to get hold of a long pole emerging from the back of the buck and bodily swing the whole mill round. This job was made easier in later mills where the sails were mounted on a rotating cap at the top of a fixed tower.

In popular mythology the miller was often seen as a dishonest fellow. No one could ever be quite certain how much flour they would get from the grain they delivered to the mill, and anyone who got less than they expected automatically assumed the miller had taken more than his fair share. In *The Canterbury Tales*, Chaucer's miller in 'The

◄ The millstones and gearing of Moxey Mill, Northamptonshire, built at the end of the 18th century.

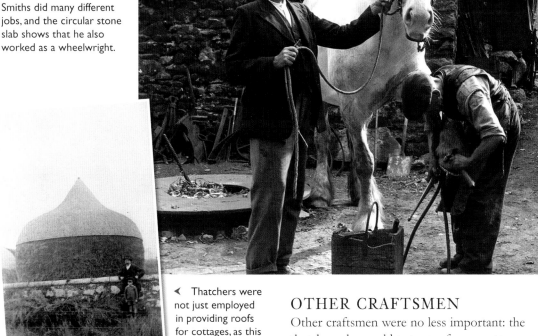

> ➤ A blacksmith at work. Smiths did many different jobs, and the circular stone slab shows that he also worked as a wheelwright.

◄ Thatchers were not just employed in providing roofs for cottages, as this beautifully thatched rick demonstrates.

Reeve's Tale' was described as being 'proud as any peacock' and 'a thief of corn'. But grumble as the farmers might, the miller was an indispensable member of the community.

THE BLACKSMITH

Apart from the grain mill, the other essential building in any community was the smithy or forge. The name 'blacksmith' simply indicates that a man works with iron as opposed to a tinsmith, for example. If he specialized in shoeing horses then he was a farrier, but most smiths did far more than that. They could make and repair simple farm machinery, or make a hinge for a gate or a link for a chain. In the early years of the motorcar if, as was not unusual given the roads at the time, a driver broke his back axle, the smith would forge him a new one.

OTHER CRAFTSMEN

Other craftsmen were no less important: the thatcher who could put a roof on a cottage or cover a hayrick for winter; the saddler who provided the harness for the working horses. These people were as much a part of farming life as the shepherd and the ploughman.

▲ Saddler Jim Bousfield at work on a harness.

▲ Children picking potatoes in the 1940s.

SEVEN PENNIES FOR SEVEN PECKS

Seasonal work provided employment for very large numbers. A Nottinghamshire farmer, recorded in the 19th century, employed 400–500 women and children to pull peas each year. It was hard work pulling the plants, either stooping down or working on hands and knees, collecting peas in their aprons and then emptying them into baskets or sacks. They were paid by volume not weight, using the old measure of a peck – two gallons or nine litres. A good worker could pick seven pecks a day, which would earn them 7d (3p).

There were times in the farming year when extra hands were needed. Fruit needed picking when it was ripe: root crops such as potatoes had to be lifted when they were ready. A Parliamentary report on the employment of women and children in agriculture, produced in 1867–68, gives a good deal of evidence on the lives of seasonal workers.

FRUIT AND VEGETABLE PICKING

In areas such as the Vale of Evesham in Worcestershire, many families were employed in the fruit harvest, mostly women and children. They were particularly in demand for picking currants as men were considered far too clumsy and likely to damage the fruit. The women would arrive at the farm with their own baskets,

▲ Preserving potatoes by packing them in straw to make a clamp.

and they and their children would be paid as a single unit, depending on how much fruit they had picked.

Among the toughest jobs was picking root vegetables. Diarist A. J. Munby, writing in the 1860s, described the 'strong women' working at Plumstead Marshes in south-east London: 'It was refreshing to see them rising from their knees in the furrows where they had crawled nearly the whole day, and trooping to the roads, wheeling empty barrows or striding along with their fustian jackets over their arms.'

Lifting vegetables such as potatoes was not the end of the day's work. They had to be stored and kept for a long time. This was normally done by clamping. A shallow hole was dug and filled with straw. The potatoes were left to dry out for an hour so that their skins hardened, then they were piled up in a pyramid. When the clamp was full, the vegetables were covered with another layer of straw and then topped with earth. A hole, stuffed with straw, was left in the top of the clamp for ventilation. Stored like this, potatoes could be kept right through the winter.

➤ Hop pickers in Kent, in the early 1900s.

HOP PICKING

For one urban group, the farm work was considered not so much a chore as a country holiday with pay. They were families from London's East End who headed off each summer for the hop fields of Kent. There were two distinct periods of work. The first was from the end of April to early June, when poles were erected for the hop bine to climb. Tying the hops was women's work, as an article in the *Agricultural Gazette* of 1864 explained: 'Tying hops is very pleasant work for women when the weather is fine: they earn from 1s 6d to 2s [7.5p to 10p] per day at this work, which requires dexterity in fastening the rushes around the tender heads of the bines, not too tight to stop their progress upwards, nor too loose as to allow them to slip back again.'

In September the great influx of workers came for the harvest. In the 1860s it was estimated that around 160,000 workers descended on Kent, many of them coming back year after year. The Parliamentary report of the 1860s noted that this was very much a family affair, the mother arriving with 'five or six children, and varying from those who are bordering on manhood to the infant who is rolled in a shawl or sack and laid upon the ground at the mother's feet'.

THE AGE OF THE TRACTOR

The first major changes in providing new sources of power came in Germany at the end of the 19th century. In 1892 Rudolf Diesel took out a patent for an internal combustion engine, using oil as a fuel. It was not long before two other brilliant engineers, Gottlieb Daimler of Württemberg and Karl Benz of Mannheim, had adapted this engine to use as transport, for motor cars and motorcycles. In America two companies took the lead in bringing the new technology to agriculture by building tractors. The International Harvester Company (IHC) was formed in 1902 from a number of manufacturers of agricultural machinery, including McCormick, who had introduced the first mechanical reaper. It was almost inevitable that the man who had brought mass production to the car industry with his Model T would get involved:

Henry Ford began turning out the Fordson tractor in 1916. It was lightweight and affordable, even for use on comparatively small farms. It was ideal for America where oil was plentiful and cheap, but was not so readily taken up in Britain at first.

FEWER FARMHANDS

The First World War brought immense changes to British society. With so many men going into the armed forces and a need to increase production with fewer hands, the government began a programme to encourage farmers to turn to tractors. Between 1914 and 1919 around 3,000 IHC Mogul or Titan tractors were imported into Britain.

The tractor could do everything the steam traction engine could – and more. Because it was so much lighter than the traction engine it caused less

▼ An early tractor and reaper, photographed in the first decade of the 20th century.

damage to the ground and the benefit could be increased even further by using either caterpillar treads or, later, pneumatic tyres to spread the load. The first victim of the tractor was the steam plough. In the older system, there was a whole team of men needed to work the two engines and guide the plough. At first the tractor was simply used as a replacement for a team of horses, so the plough still needed to be steered. It was a farmer's son from Ireland, Harry Ferguson, who saw that there was an alternative. He was both an inventive and adventurous young man: at the age of 25 he designed, built and flew his own aeroplane. In 1917 he designed a rigid combination of plough and tractor – though the tractor was only an old Model T Ford. Eventually he was to go into partnership with Ford and in the 1930s Ferguson tractors were being made at Dagenham, Essex.

REPLACING THE HEAVY HORSE

The rigid system meant that one man could control both the tractor and whatever implement was attached, such as plough or harrow. It was a versatile machine that could do many jobs on the farm. It could be used instead of a heavy horse, and it could also be used as a stationary engine to work machines such as threshers and grain elevators. It was the start of a new phase in agriculture. Soon other improvements were made, including the self-lifting plough introduced by the former traction-engine makers Ransome in 1919. But change was slow. George Garrard, who farmed in Suffolk, was working

▲ The old and the new: a tractor is being used as a stationary engine to operate the elevator, but horses were still being used to pull the cart in this 1940s scene.

with six horses when he bought his first tractor, 'a big owd thing that drew a three-furrow plough. There were only about half a dozen of them in the county'. He sold two of his horses, then bought a Fordson and sold two more horses, and continued working with two tractors and two horses right up to 1939. It was just as well he kept those horses, for with the outbreak of war fuel was to become a precious commodity.

➤ International Mogul tractors such as this were imported from America during the First World War to boost production.

Women had always worked on the farm in a wide variety of tasks, but the two world wars of the 20th century saw them, for the first time, doing jobs that had previously been reserved for men. It was not that farmers' attitudes were changing, but a necessity when so many men were away at war.

THE WOMEN'S LAND ARMY

The first Women's Land Army (WLA) was formed in 1917 when women over the age of 18 were invited to volunteer for general farm work. Popularly known as land girls, they were given six weeks training and once they had passed a proficiency test they were paid £1 a week. It was not just that they were often doing men's work that caused a certain amount of controversy, they were also provided with a uniform that included a pair of breeches, which was considered almost

Second World War recruitment poster.

scandalous. The young women either lived on the farm or were billeted on farm workers, and a few lived in special hostels. By the time they were disbanded in 1919 some 10,000 women had been taken on, but very few remained in their jobs when the men came back from war.

At the start of the Second World War in 1939 the need for British agriculture to increase production was of paramount importance. With the German U-boats attacking merchant ships, the country could no longer rely on imported grain and the government forced many farmers to turn pasture over to arable farming. Once again there was a

◄ Many of the young women in the WLA found themselves still using age-old techniques, such as sowing by hand.

THE RUNAWAY
LAND GIRL

As a 17-year-old in 1945, Jeanne-Marie Titchiner (née Parsons) answered Prime Minister Clement Atlee's call to join the WLA. She recounts how her time at a dairy farm near Fleet, Hampshire, came to an abrupt end: 'I failed to stop the determined bull bursting into the milking parlour and squeezing himself into a pen, refusing to budge. It took four angry men over an hour to remove him. Was I in disgrace! That night, under cover of darkness, I piled all my belongings onto my bicycle and wheeled it the three miles to the station, and headed home on the milk train.'

▲ Jeanne-Marie Parsons mastering the milking machine. Despite her initial naivety, resulting in numerous rebukes from an exasperated herdsman for the slightest mistake, she came to enjoy many farm tasks, including haymaking and harvesting.

shortage of manpower and the WLA was re-formed. The women were required to work a maximum of 50 hours a week in summer and 48 in winter and for this they received just over £1 a week, once money had been deducted for board and lodging. As one worker said, the only entertainment she could afford was a visit to the cinema once a week and a sing-along with the other girls in the hostel after work.

Some of the more conservative farmers were reluctant to admit that the women could do men's work and used them as domestic servants instead of field hands. But in time they discovered that these young women, even if they had come from towns and cities, were more than capable of handling any job on the farm that came their way. The WLA was only disbanded in 1950, by which time 90,000 women had worked on Britain's farms.

THE POST-WAR YEARS

After the war, men drifted back to the farms, but life was changing. Increasing mechanization meant that fewer hands were needed. To use the new machines more effectively, old hedges were dug up, walls knocked down and fields enlarged. Features that had for centuries been a familiar part of the farming scene vanished: the haystack gave way to the plastic-bound bundle of silage. Life on the farm has been transformed forever, but we cannot lose sight of the fact that pre-war farming was a far from romantic era – the work was back-breaking, the hours long and conditions often far from pleasant. New methods resulted in increased yields, but many farmers have now turned away from the extensive use of artificial fertilizers and the rearing of animals in factory-like conditions. Once again cattle roam the fields and hens peck happily around the farmyard.

NFU

The National Farmers Union was formed in 1908 to represent the interest of farmers. It has been involved in the passing of many laws, including the Corn Production Repeal Act (1912), the Wool Marketing Act (1950), the Control of Pollution Act (1974), and the Countryside and Rights of Way Act (2000).

PLACES TO VISIT

Many farms are open to the public as visitor attractions and a list can be found at www.farmattractions.net. The following farms and museums are of historic as well as general interest. Contact them or visit their websites for further information, including details of opening dates and times.

Aberdeenshire Farming Museum, Aden Country Park, Mintlaw, Peterhead, Aberdeenshire AB42 5FQ

Acton Scott Working Farm, near Church Stretton, Shropshire SY6 6QQ

Beamish: the Living Museum of the North, Beamish, County Durham DH9 0RG

Chillingham Wild Cattle Association, Chillingham, Alnwick, Northumberland NE66 5NP

Chiltern Open Air Museum, Newland Park, Gorelands Lane, Chalfont St Giles, Buckinghamshire HP8 4AB

Cogges Farm, Cogges, Witney, Oxfordshire OX28 3LA

Corrigall Farm Museum, Harray, Orkney KW17 2JR

Cotswold Farm Park, Guiting Power, near Cheltenham, Gloucestershire GL54 5UG

Dairyland Farm World, Newquay, Cornwall TR8 5AA

Denny Abbey Farmland Museum, Ely Road, Waterbeach, Cambridge CB25 9PQ

▲ Harnessing heavy horses at the Yorkshire Museum of Farming.

Ewe-Phoria, Llangwm, Cerrigydrudion, Denbighshire LL21 0RE

Gressenhall Farm and Workhouse, Gressenhall, Dereham, Norfolk NR20 4DR

Kent Life, Lock Lane, Sandling, Maidstone, Kent ME14 3AU

Laidhay Croft Museum, Laidhay, Dunbeath, Caithness KW6 6EH

Manor Farm and Country Park, Pylands Lane, Bursledon, Southampton, Hampshire SO31 1BH

Museum of East Anglian Life, Iliffe Way, Stowmarket, Suffolk IP14 1DL

Museum of English Rural Life, University of Reading, Redlands Road, Reading, Berkshire RG1 5EX

The Museum of Lincolnshire Life, Burton Road, Lincoln LN1 3LY

The National Folk Museum at Cregneash, Cregneash Road, Cregneash, Isle of Man IM9 5PX

National Museum of Rural Life Scotland, Wester Kittochside, Philipshill Road, East Kilbride, South Lanarkshire G76 9HR

Sacrewell Farm and Country Centre, Thornhaugh, Peterborough, Cambridgeshire PE8 6HJ

Seven Sisters Sheep Centre, Gilberts Drive, East Dean, East Sussex BN20 0AA

Shetland Crofthouse Museum, Boddam, Dunrossness, Shetland ZE2 9JQ

St Fagans: National History Museum, Cardiff Road, Cardiff CF5 6XB

The Village Church Farm, Church Road South, Skegness, Lincolnshire PE25 2HF

Wayside Museum, Zennor, St Ives, Cornwall TR26 3DA

Weald and Downland Open Air Museum, Town Lane, Singleton, Chichester, West Sussex PO18 0EU

Wimpole Estate: Home Farm, Arrington, Royston, Cambridgeshire SG8 0BW

Yorkshire Museum of Farming, Murton, York YO19 5UF

Information correct at time of going to press.